Johannes Brahms

QUINTET AND QUARTETS FOR PIANO AND STRINGS

From the Breitkopf & Härtel Complete Works Edition

Edited by Hans Gál

DOVER PUBLICATIONS, INC.
New York

CONTENTS

Copyright © 1985 by Dover Publications, Inc.
All rights reserved under Pan American and International Copyright Conventions.

Published in Canada by General Publishing Company, Ltd., 30 Lesmill Road, Don Mills, Toronto, Ontario.

Published in the United Kingdom by Constable and Company, Ltd., 10 Orange Street, London WC2H 7EG.

This Dover edition, first published in 1985, is an unabridged republication of Volume 8 (*Klavier-Quintett und -Quartette*) of *Johannes Brahms; Sämtliche Werke; Ausgabe der Gesellschaft der Musikfreunde in Wien,* originally published by Breitkopf & Härtel, Leipzig, n.d. (Editor's Commentary dated Summer 1927). The Editor's Commentary was translated by Stanley Appelbaum specially for the present edition.

Manufactured in the United States of America
Dover Publications, Inc., 31 East 2nd Street, Mineola, N.Y. 11501

Library of Congress Cataloging in Publication Data

Brahms, Johannes, 1833-1897.
   [Chamber music. Selections]
   Quintet and quartets for piano and strings.

   Reprint. Originally published: Leipzig : Breitkopf & Härtel, 1927. (Sämtliche Werke / Johannes Brahms ; Bd. 8) With new English translation of the editorial commentary.
   Contents: Quintet for piano and strings in F minor, op. 34—Quartet no. 1 for piano and strings in G minor, op. 25—Quartet no. 2 for piano and strings in A major, op. 26—[etc.]
   1. Piano quintets—Scores. 2. Piano quartets—Scores. I. Gál, Hans, 1890-
II. Brahms, Johannes, 1833-1897. Quintets, piano, strings, op. 34, F minor, 1985.
III. Brahms, Johannes, 1833-1897. Quartets, piano, strings, 1985.
M178.B7G3 1985   85-750706
ISBN 0-486-24900-X

EDITOR'S COMMENTARY

QUINTET IN F MINOR, OP. 34

SOURCE TEXTS:
1. The C. F. Peters edition.
2. Brahms's personal working copy of the original Rieter-Biedermann edition, in the possession of the Gesellschaft der Musikfreunde in Vienna.

COMMENTS:

The Quintet was published in 1865 by Rieter-Biedermann with the title "Quintett für Pianoforte, zwei Violinen, Viola und Violoncell componirt von Johannes Brahms. Op. 34," publication number 435. On the inside title page: "Dedicated to her Royal Highness Princess Anna of Hessen." The newly engraved C. F. Peters edition of 1919 follows the original edition, but the original is more reliable with regard to bowing phrases and the like. Brahms's personal working copy contains two insignificant corrections of engraving errors, but no other entry. Aside from a few further engraving errors (the only one conspicuous among them is a *B*-sharp instead of *B*-natural in m. 436 of the Finale in the piano upper staff), Source Text 2 is thoroughly unobjectionable.

The work originated in 1862 as a string quintet, was next reworked in the winter 1863/4 as the sonata for two pianos later published as Op. 34b, and then received its present, definitive form as a piano quintet in the summer of 1864. The original string quintet version was not published and was later destroyed by Brahms. (See Kalbeck's biography of Brahms, vol. II, pp. 52 ff.)

QUARTET NO. 1 IN G MINOR, OP. 25

SOURCE TEXTS:
1. The Simrock printed edition (full score and string parts).
2. Brahms's personal working copy, in the possession of the Gesellschaft der Musikfreunde in Vienna.
3. The original MS, in the possession of W. Kux, Vienna.

COMMENTS:

The work was published by N. Simrock in 1863. The original title reads: "Quartett für Pianoforte, Violine Viola und Violoncello componirt und Herrn Baron Reinhard von Dalwigk zugeeignet von Johannes Brahms Op. 25," publication number 6264.

The original edition contains a number of engraving errors and inaccuracies, some of which are corrected in the personal working copy, and some of which were able to be corrected by comparison either with the MS or, for the string instruments, with the more reliable printed string parts. The plate divisions marked off on the original MS show that it was used as the engraving copy. The title on the MS corresponds exactly with the printed one. At the end is the dating: "Johannes Brahms Sept. 1861." The Intermezzo originally bore the indication "Scherzo." The MS also shows numerous alterations that were later adopted; the most interesting of these is the deletion of a 19-measure interlude in the third movement. This deleted passage occurred between the present mm. 206 and 207 of the Andante, and read as follows:

iv

continuation as in the
printed edition, m. 208

v

QUARTET NO. 2 IN A MAJOR, OP. 26

SOURCE TEXTS:
1. The Simrock edition.
2. Brahms's personal working copy of the score, in the possession of the Gesellschaft der Musikfreunde in Vienna.

COMMENTS:

The work was published in 1863 by N. Simrock with the title "Quartett für Pianoforte, Violine, Viola und Violoncello componirt von Johannes Brahms Op. 26," publication number 6259. The edition contains a number of unimportant engraving errors, some of which are corrected in the personal working copy, especially small inaccuracies in the string parts. In m. 8 of the [Poco] Adagio, the piano upper staff has a decidedly incorrect natural sign in front of the grace note *f*-sharp. On the basis of the most probable assumption, it has been changed here to a double-sharp, but it should be observed that when this passage recurs in mm. 31, 93 and 134 (not in the piano, of course, but in the strings) there is always a simple *f*-sharp.

QUARTET NO. 3 IN C MINOR, OP. 60

SOURCE TEXTS:
1. The Simrock edition.
2. Brahms's personal working copy of the score, in the possession of the Gesellschaft der Musikfreunde in Vienna.
3. The original MS of the last movement, in the possession of the Gesellschaft der Musikfreunde in Vienna.

COMMENTS:

The work was published in 1875 by N. Simrock. The original title reads: "Quartett c moll für Pianoforte, Violine, Bratsche und Violoncell von Johannes Brahms. Op. 60," publication number 7702. The edition is practically free of errors; the personal working copy contains a single entry, the pedal notation in mm. 4 and 16 of the first movement.

In m. 90 of the Andante the last eighth-beat for the viola has *e/d* in the original edition instead of *e/c*-sharp.

Hans Gál

Vienna, Summer 1927

Quintet
for Piano and Strings in F Minor
Op. 34

Scherzo

Trio

Scherzo *D. C. sin' al Fine*

un pochettino più animato

un pochettino più animato

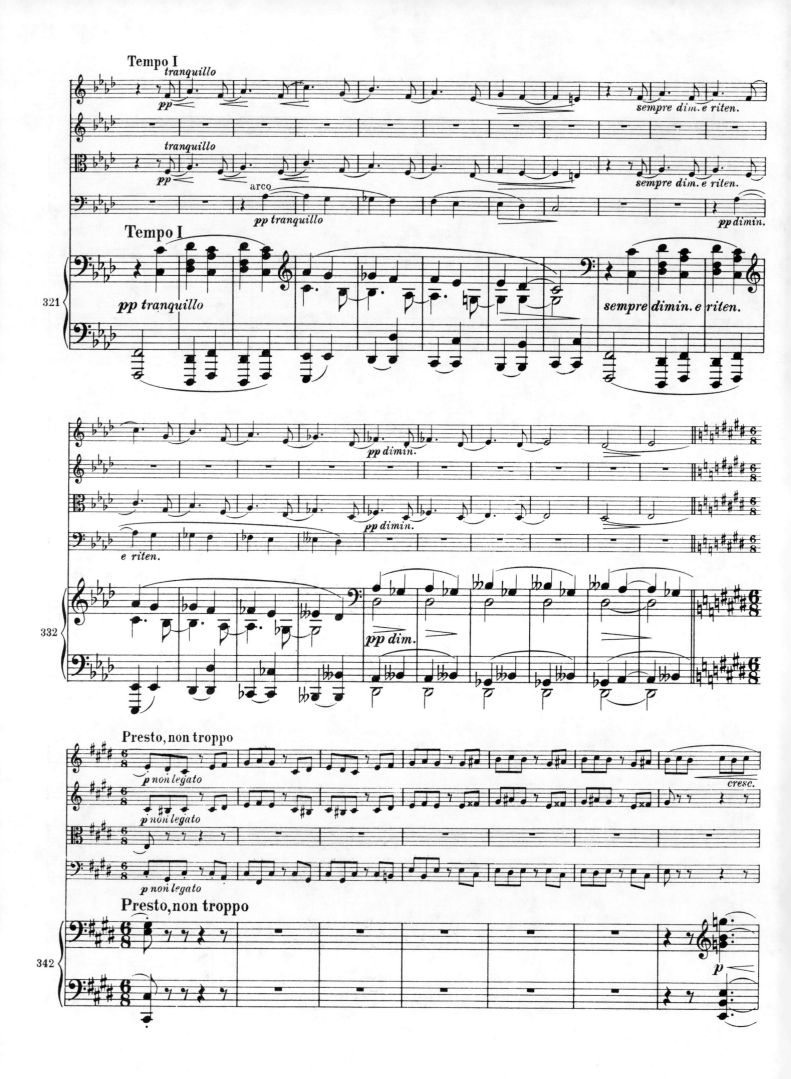

Quartet No. 1
for Piano and Strings in G Minor
Op. 25

Intermezzo

Allegro, ma non troppo

★ The frequency of the use of *una corda* in the Intermezzo and its Trio is left to the judgment of the player.

Trio

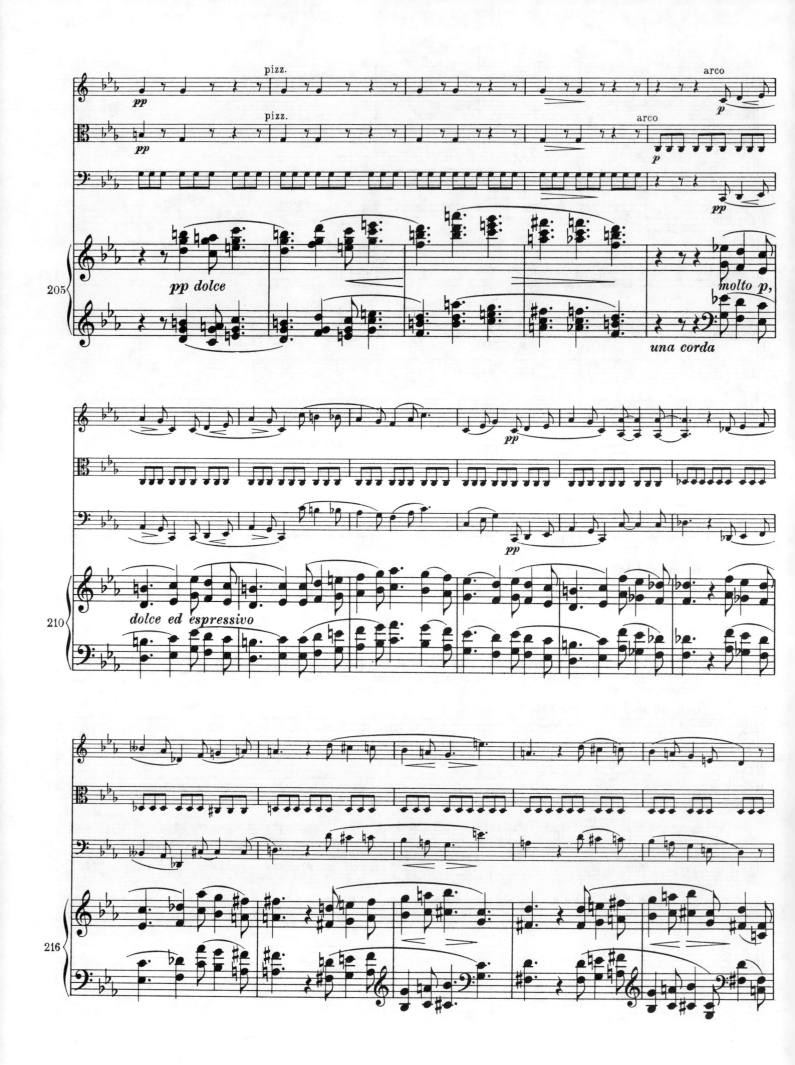

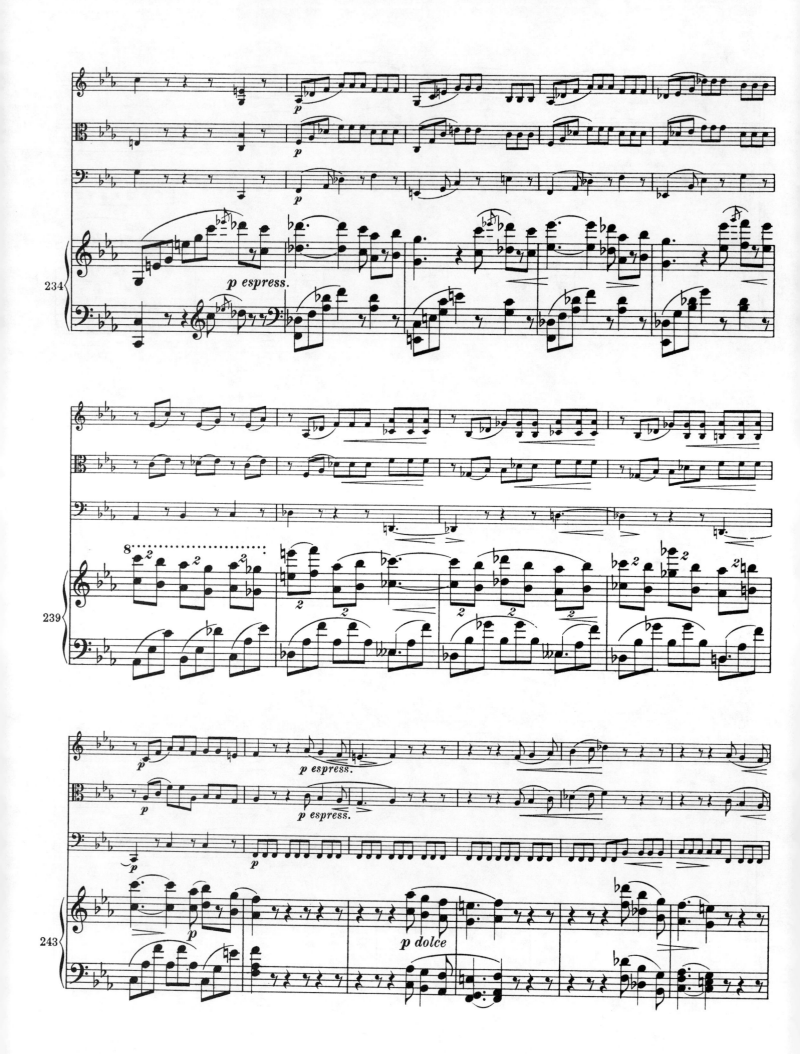

Coda

Animato

Rondo alla Zingarese

Quartet No. 2
for Piano and Strings in A Major
Op. 26

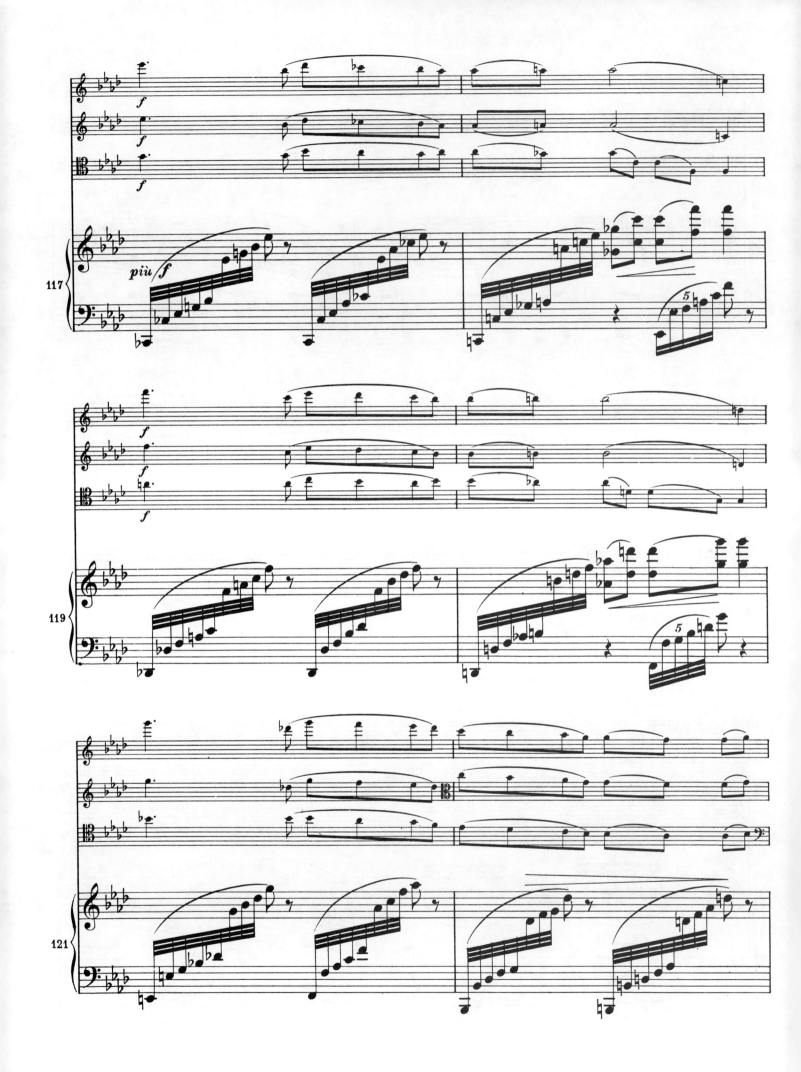

Trio

Scherzo da Capo senza repl. sin al Fine

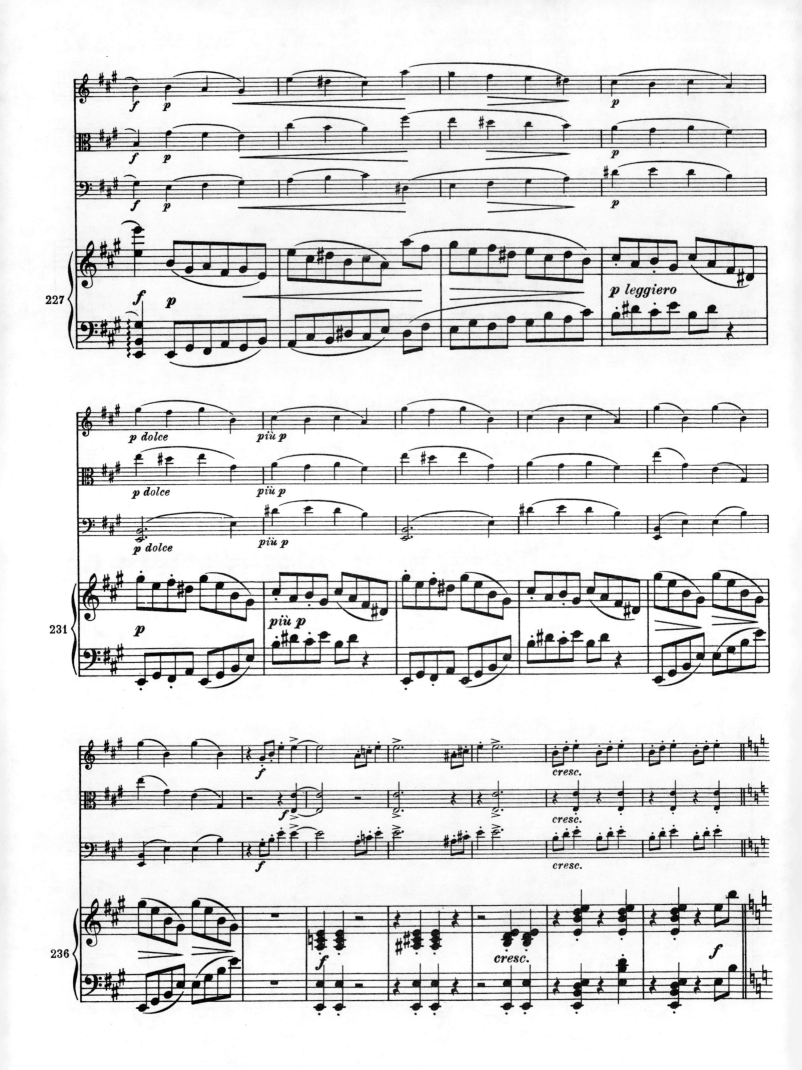

Quartet No. 3
for Piano and Strings in C Minor
Op. 60

244   QUARTET NO. 3 IN C MINOR, OP. 60

Quartet No. 3 in C Minor, Op. 60

254 QUARTET NO. 3 IN C MINOR, OP. 60

Scherzo

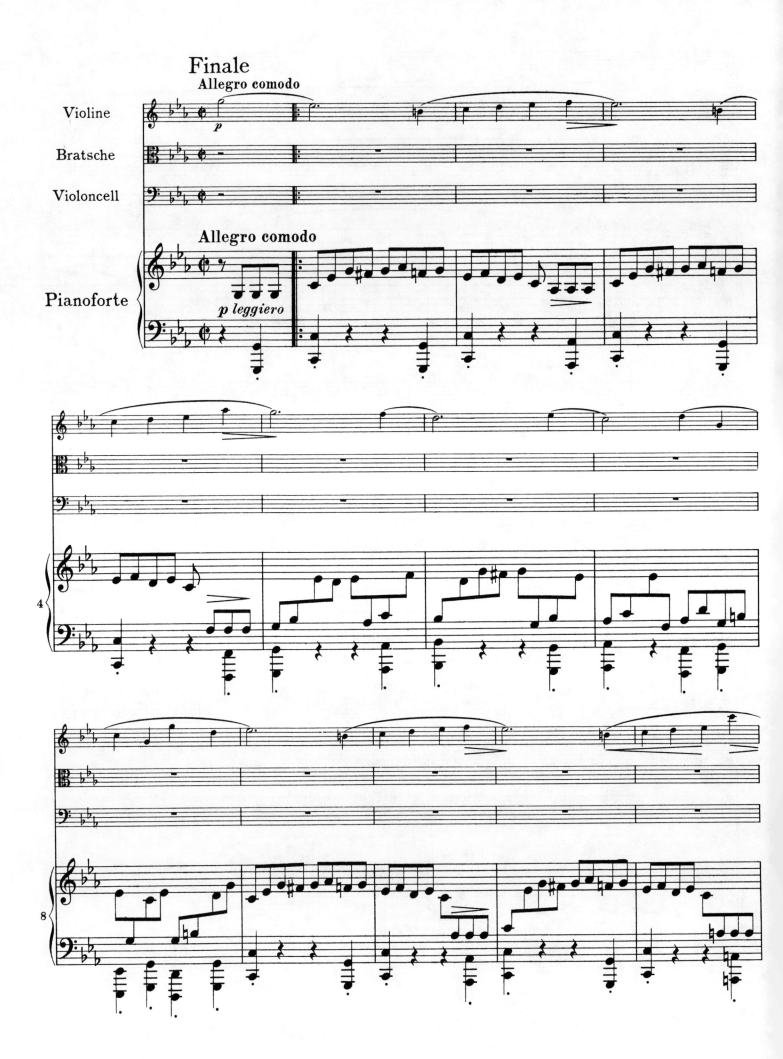

Quartet No. 3 in C Minor, Op. 60

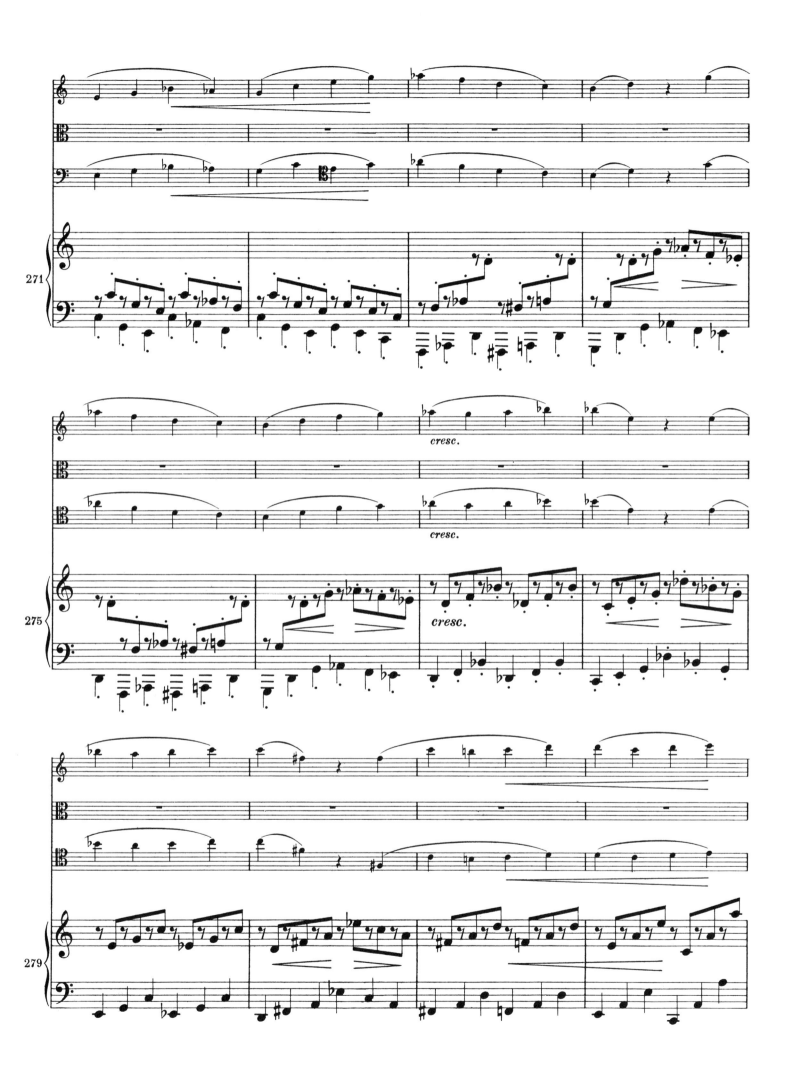

Quartet No. 3 in C Minor, Op. 60